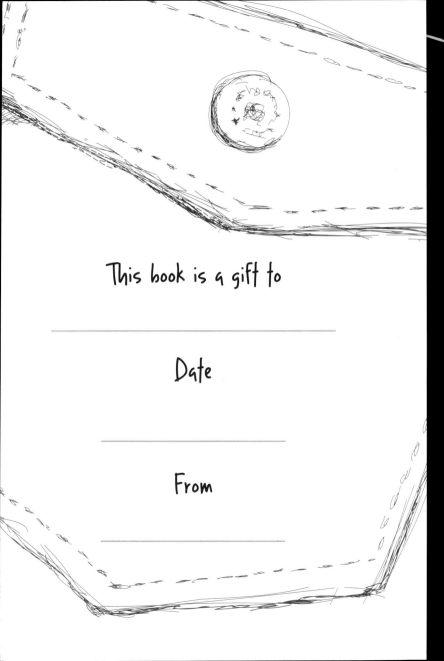

This book is a gift to

_____

Date

_____

From

_____

Blessings from God for Teens

© 2012 Christian Art Gifts, RSA
       Christian Art Gifts Inc., IL, USA

Designed by Christian Art Gifts

Images used under license from Shutterstock.com

Printed in China

ISBN 978-1-77036-643-5

12 13 14 15 16 17 18 19 20 21 – 10 9 8 7 6 5 4 3 2 1

BLESSINGS
FROM GOD FOR
TEENS

Karen Moore

christian
art gifts®

GOD'S BLESSINGS JUST FOR YOU!!!

Your life is changing! Everything you know is churning and turning and burning a new trail and you're doing your best to keep up with it.

Your friends are strange and wonderful in the ways they act and the things they do. Some of them shape your thinking, some help you grow. Some friends just keep you puzzled. Like it or not, friends guide you in great ways or they influence you in goofy ways. The good news is that you're in the game, giving life your best shot. You're in it to win it because there's a lot more up ahead.

The Game Is On, Try Again!

You're trying hard,
You're moving fast,
You're wondering if
This game can last.
Once again,
You're up at bat,
A swing, a miss
You're falling flat.
But wait,
You've got another chance,
You win, you score,
It's time to dance!

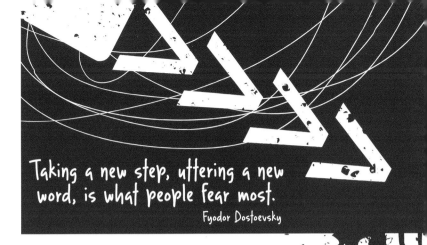

> Taking a new step, uttering a new word, is what people fear most.
>
> Fyodor Dostoevsky

You're setting a new course … growing up, maybe driving a car, perhaps dating, setting a future goal, thinking about what you want to become, discovering some boundaries, taking some risks and it's all good. What makes it better is that you have everything you need to navigate the waters ahead. You're surrounded by people who care about you. Even more, you are a teenager in the hands of the God of the Universe. You were formed and shaped by His hand and **YOU ARE BLESSED** and known and loved right where you stand.

YOU'RE *NOT* ALONE.

Read on for a taste of inspiration, ideas to ponder and motivate your direction, and little prayers to keep you steady. It's cool to be you and what's more, it's cool for you to connect with the Creator of the Universe, the One who set the stars in motion. This same Creator has stood by your side from the moment you beamed on to planet Earth. It's time to understand more fully the blessings from God … meant just for you.

To change your life, take these steps.

1. Start immediately, there's no reason to wait.
2. Do it flamboyantly, that means with energy, excitement and joy. It's your whole life we're talking about here.
3. Don't make excuses. Make God proud! "I know the plans I have for you," declares the LORD, "plans to prosper you and not to harm you, plans to give you hope and a future" (Jer. 29:11).

    God has planned a lot of good things for you, so hang on, fasten your seat belt and get ready for the ride of your life. It's going to be full of ups and downs and more twists and turns than a roller coaster, but you're safe, locked in by invisible forces. Put up your hands and shout for joy!

The LORD is like a father to His children, tender and compassionate to those who fear Him. For He understands how weak we are; He knows we are only dust.

Psalm 103:13-14 NLT

Cool Thought:
You don't choose your family. They are God's gift to you, as you are to them.
Desmond Tutu

Who Made the Rules, Anyway?

You, Your Family, and the Rules

No doubt your family has its own culture, its own vibe, or unique way of doing things. The rules of your house may be different from the rules your friends live by in their houses. All across the world, kids are growing up, trying to figure out how to be responsible teens and goal-oriented adults.

GIFTS OF FAMILY

Character is better than ancestry, and personal conduct is more important than the highest form of parenting. Your roots matter, but what you do with the gifts you're given by ancestry is all up to you.

Thomas John Barnardo

What Will Be Your Rules for Living a Great Life?

Your rules for life are being formed right where you stand. You may be growing up with great rules, the kind you respect and find fairly easy to follow. You may be growing up with no rules and you're wondering why. You may think you have too many rules, but the good news is you're growing. You're learning about yourself, who you are in the context of your family and who you are at school. In more ways than you realize, you are actually creating some of your own rules.

Parents can only give good advice
or put you on the right paths,
but the final forming of your character
lies in your own hands. Anne Frank

You're already deciding what you value, what matters, what you think it feels like to have good friends or fun relationships. As you decide these things, you let go of others that you've learned don't work very well for you. Sure, you make mistakes as you go, but that's all part of the learning process. That's what gives you the courage to keep trying and it's what helps you see that God knows you're there.

Your Life Is God's Gift to You.
Your Gift to Him Is What You Do with This Life!

This time in your life is God's blessing to you. This place where you live with your family, no matter how they are structured, is a gift to you. You are on the way to discovering who you want to be and who God wants you to be. What feels right and safe and comfortable is being set in your heart today. You're on a path designed with purpose and great love. Step forward with caution, with joy, and with trust. The One who made you is right by your side whenever you invite Him to be there.

Tips/Advice:

Look at the rules you live by today. What would you change? What would you keep? What rules help you understand a little more of what life is all about? Make a list of the rules you think are cool and the ones you think are lame. Now take out the word "rules" and replace it with something that helps you live with the rules more easily ... maybe calling them "tips for life" or "guidelines" or "my navigation tools". You can name them whatever you like.

They're part of the blessing; part of God's roadmap to help you along the paths of life.

DEAR GOD, I don't always like the rules of my house. Sometimes I just want to have things my way. Please help me to see Your hand in shaping and guiding me as I grow. Help me to be a cool follower of You. **AMEN.**

Families are like fudge ... mostly sweet with a few nuts.

Anonymous

FATHERS, MOTHERS, AND OTHER ALIENS

Even though you have ten thousand guardians in Christ, you do not have many fathers, for in Christ Jesus I became your father through the gospel.

1 Corinthians 4:15 NIV

Cool Thought:
Your parents were once teenagers. They were on unfamiliar ground too, learning to listen to voices of authority and learning to step out into the world on their own. Once, they were right where you are now!

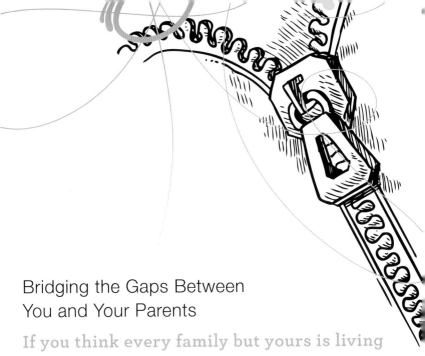

Bridging the Gaps Between
You and Your Parents

If you think every family but yours is living an ideal lifestyle, **think again.** Whether you have both parents at home, or both parents living separately, or just Mom or just Dad, you have to learn how to understand each other, how to grow up together. It can seem like you're from two very different worlds.

In some ways, you are.

Understanding Your Parents

Your parents are God's gift to you, trying to point the way, trying to help you avoid mistakes that they made at your age, trying to make sure your needs are met. If your parents seem like aliens more than they seem like gifts at times, you might need to look in the mirror to see how many eyes you have in the back of your head. **How you see each other depends on how good your ears are.** That's right! How well you listen to each other makes a huge difference in your ability to see things as they are intended.

What's the best way to communicate with aliens, I mean with parents, or those in authority over you? **Here are some helpful hints:**

Pick the right time to talk. If Dad just came home from a grueling day or Mom's boss just loaded more work on

her than she knows how to handle, a discussion the moment they walk in the door, may not be a good idea. Be wise, let everybody chill a bit, maybe even wait till dinner time to try for meaningful conversation. In fact, offer to help make dinner or set the table.

Think it through first. If you want to ask permission to go to a party on Friday night, then be ready with the details. How will you get there? Who will be there? Will there be any alcohol or drugs? Will there be a chaperone? The more answers you can provide, the more comfortable your parents will be about giving you the freedom to attend the party. Be ready to share with your parents why it's important to you to be able to go to the party.

Watch Your Thoughts

Watch your thoughts, for they become words.
Watch your words, for they become actions.
Watch your actions, for they become habits.
Watch your habits, for they become character.
Watch your character, for it becomes your destiny!

Be responsible. This is a tricky one because you may not consciously want to take responsibility for your actions. You may want your parents to bail you out if something goes wrong or if things don't go as planned. If you're going to have successful conversations about any topic that requires approval from your parents, you will want to offer your own bit of wisdom and show your willingness to be responsible for the things you want to do.

Stop and look at swinging moods. If you were all set to try to talk, but your mom has a severe headache from a hard day, or your dad is blowing up because his favorite team missed the winning field goal, you might want to step to the side and wait till the air is clear again. This goes for your mood too. Of course, you're never moody, but if it should happen that you are, even for a moment, remember to dial it down till later.

Be polite. It always works best if you present your side of any story in a way that shows respect for your elders. It gives them the chance to respect you right back. It gives you both a way to be comfortable in the process.

Another Cool Thought:

Be Careful How You Speak to Others.

God has given us two ears, but one tongue, to show that we should be swift to hear, but slow to speak. God has set a double fence before the tongue, the teeth and the lips, to teach us to be wary that we offend not with our tongue.

Thomas Watson

Relax and be yourself. By this time, you all know each other pretty well. Circumstances may have changed over time or you may be working with some new material (they may not be ready to know you're old enough to drive or get a job after school). Sometimes parents miss those things, but if you are your wonderful self, honest and honorable, you'll have talks that get the results you hope for. You'll be ready to take some big steps.

Your Heavenly Father Is Always Ready to Listen to YOU.

So, talking to people who don't seem to be exactly on the same page you are, can be tricky, but you have another tool in your box to help you discuss anything. You can take whatever is on your mind to God in prayer. You can put everything before Him and when you have a sense of peace in your heart, you'll know you've got what you need to make things happen.

God's blessing to you is continually there, always something you can count on because you are important to Him. First Peter 5:6-7 says, "Humble yourselves, therefore, under God's mighty hand, that He may lift you up in due time. Cast all your anxiety on Him because He cares for you."

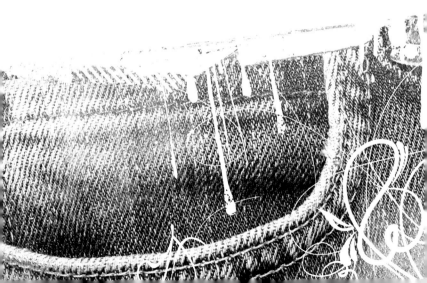

Tips/Advice:

Spend some time with your parents. Get to know what they were like when they were your age. What worries did they have? Who did they talk to when they had problems? What did they do for fun?

The more you know about them and the more you remind them of those days, the more they will understand you. You'll have common ground to work things out together. You can help them to step back into your shoes for just a little while and if you can, try to step into their shoes too. You'll all get along a lot easier.

DEAR GOD, in spite of how much I can talk to my friends, sometimes I just don't know how to talk to my parents about things. They never have enough time, or they don't seem to understand what I'm going through, or I simply don't know how to explain what I'm feeling and thinking. Please help me to share my heart with them in ways that make it easier for us to keep all the lines of communication open.

Thanks for listening! **AMEN.**

Even God struggles with whether people listen to Him. There's a roadside sign which says,

"If you listen to Me now,
I won't have to shout later." God.

SIBLINGS, SQUABBLES, AND SPLITTING A PIZZA

Starting a quarrel is like breaching a dam;
so drop the matter before a dispute breaks out.

Proverbs 17:14

This probably doesn't happen to you, but believe it or not, some brothers and sisters don't get along. Sometimes they actually make each other crazy. They compare, compete, complain, control, confuse, and otherwise create anything but a cool space where they can just hang out in peace.

Whew! Wouldn't it be better to be battling it out over a cool video game, or stunning each other with brilliance in a board game? Wouldn't it be better to be splitting a pizza?

There's a rule somewhere that says,

"Life actually gets better with a pepperoni pizza!"

Great tranquility

(that is peace of mind and of heart)

belongs to

anyone who cares

for neither praise

nor blame.

Adapted from Thomas à Kempis

Cain and Abel

The Bible gives an example of brothers who simply couldn't get along. One brother worked at gardening and growing things and the other one took care of flocks of sheep. Abel always picked the best of his flock to give back to God and his offering pleased God. Cain was more careless about what he brought in from the garden and God did not respect his offering. That made Cain jealous of his brother. In fact, in a fit of rage, Cain killed his brother. When Cain killed Abel, he made matters worse by trying to cover it up before God. He tried to act like he didn't really know anything was wrong. God confronted Cain and he was driven away from his home and left to wander aimlessly.

"Am I my brother's keeper?" Cain asked. God seemed to think so.

What about you? Are you often left to care for younger siblings? Do you feel any responsibility toward your brother or sister? Do you wonder if you're the keeper of those in your household like Cain suggested?

God's blessing to you comes in every effort you make to build a better relationship with your brothers and sisters. God wants you to get along.

You and Your Sibling

Happily, a little argument with your sibling won't go to the extremes of Cain and Abel, but this story offers one thing worth noting. You have to be very aware of your feelings.

Look at those feelings of jealousy or competition that can sometimes erupt and be truthful to yourself about what they are and why they exist.

If you feel misunderstood, you may also feel that you're not well connected to your family. You may even feel like you're left to wander around somewhat aimlessly, even in your own house. It's possible to feel alone even when there are people around you.

Proverbs 17:14 suggests that it's really better for us to let things go, clear them up and get on with life before something even bigger erupts.

GETTING ALONG WITH YOUR SIBLINGS

Nobody should seek his own good, but the good of others.

Show you care! If you can't start with your sibling, start with yourself!

* **Be yourself** – tell the truth
* **Accept yourself** – give yourself a break
* **Value yourself** – be clear about what matters
* **Forgive yourself** – it makes it easier to forgive others too
* **Treat yourself** – do something nice just for you
* **Balance yourself** – get enough sleep, read, laugh, think, hug
* **Bless yourself** – God already blesses you, so pass on the blessings

* **Trust yourself** – have confidence in your own thoughts and ideas

* **Love yourself** – stand in front of the mirror and say something nice right to your face

* **Empower yourself** – pray, meditate, take some quiet time

* **Give of yourself** – share what you are and who you are with others; volunteer

* **Express yourself** – say what's on your mind

* **Believe in yourself** – God believes in you too

* **Enjoy yourself** – find ways to have fun

If you're confident and strong, you won't find yourself arguing over petty things with one of your brothers or sisters. You'll have better things to do. If arguments keep breaking out even when you're trying to avoid them, ask the help of a parent to guide you to a process to make things easier, or set some ground rules to communicate better. God will be pleased with your efforts.

PRACTICE KINDNESS!

**An anxious heart weighs a person down,
but a kind word cheers him up.**

Constant kindness can accomplish much. As the sun makes ice melt, kindness causes misunderstanding, mistrust and hostility to evaporate.

Albert Schweitzer

Tips/Advice:

Have you ever noticed how little things can make a difference in your day? Maybe some kid at school smiles at you and says hello, or you go home and your mom has just baked your favorite cookies. Those things that others do for you are acts of kindness. Kindness is always a win-win. Kindness is a key that opens a lot of opportunities. Try it. Do one small thing, one kind thing for someone else today, perhaps even a total stranger, and see how it feels. Make a note of it in your journal.

You'll be glad you did.

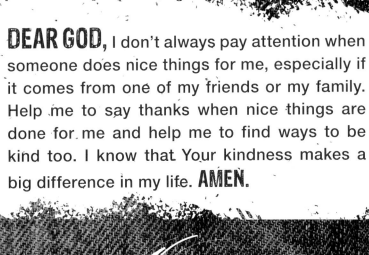

DEAR GOD, I don't always pay attention when someone does nice things for me, especially if it comes from one of my friends or my family. Help me to say thanks when nice things are done for me and help me to find ways to be kind too. I know that Your kindness makes a big difference in my life. **AMEN.**

Facing a Bull or a Bully …
It's All About the Same!

Live in harmony with one another. Romans 12:16

The first book of Samuel tells the story of David, who was taken into King Saul's house so that he could soothe him with music. When the king was feeling anxious or was just in a bad mood for some reason, music helped. You might find that music does that for you too. Anyway, David would play his harp and Saul would feel better. A little music would soothe Saul's soul. Though Saul would eventually come to bully David, he wasn't the biggest bully David ever had to face.

Giants and Other Big Bad Guys

A big bad bully named Goliath eventually appeared.
He was no ordinary bully. He was a giant over nine feet tall. He wore a coat of armor that weighed over 125 pounds. He stood and shouted insults at the army of Israel and he was relentlessly begging for a fight. The giant, Goliath, kept taunting everyone for forty, seemingly endless days.

When David heard about the bully, he decided it was time to put an end to his noisy threats. Mind you, David was a boy, perhaps a teenager, probably not more than five feet tall, lucky if he weighed 125 pounds soaking wet.

But David had one thing Goliath didn't. He had the power of the living God in his heart and mind. He believed that with God's help, he could do anything, even stop a bullying giant. **David was blessed by God because he truly believed God made all the difference.**

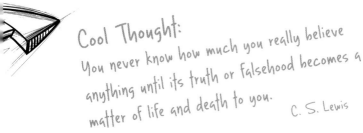

Cool Thought:
You never know how much you really believe anything until its truth or falsehood becomes a matter of life and death to you.

C. S. Lewis

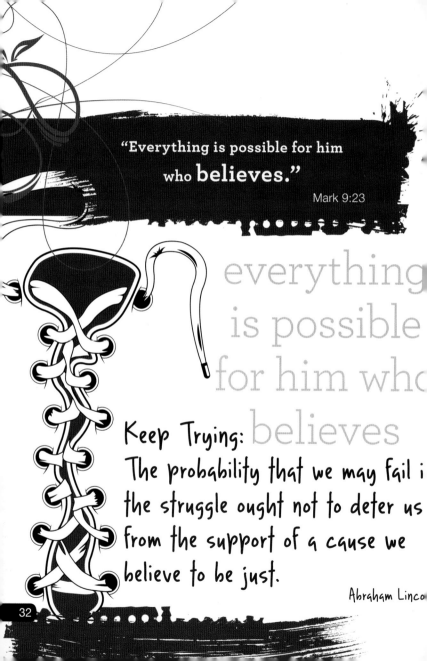

"Everything is possible for him
who **believes**."

Mark 9:23

everything
is possible
for him who

Keep Trying: believes
The probability that we may fail i
the struggle ought not to deter us
from the support of a cause we
believe to be just.

Abraham Linco

32

Bullies, Obstacles, and Struggles Come in All Shapes and Sizes

Bullies don't have to be nine feet tall. Whatever you have to confront that steals power from you, will work to make you miserable. The bullies of this world gather strength from those who feel too weak to stand up against them. They may pick on you for being too pretty, or too smart, or for not being enough of whatever they've decided is important. Bullies and personal struggles focus on your weaknesses and eat your fears for lunch.

If you are concerned about being overweight, or you happen to be biracial, or the wrong religion, or something else altogether, bullies and obstacles will show up. They will manifest as a mean spirit in some other person, or as a depressed spirit inside you and strive to break you apart. What can you do to keep these kinds of things from bugging you?

God has blessed you with His spirit.
He is with you all the time.
If you are being bullied at school
or in your community by some kind
of Goliath, there is something
you can do about it ...

Here are a few good things to keep in mind:

Stop the Bullies

- Talk about how to deal with bullies with your parents or school teachers. Let someone know what is happening
- Report any abuse from text messages or online websites
- Don't try to fight back or bully back by yourself
- Try to get other teens involved in an ongoing campus campaign to keep bullies away
- Talk to your minister or youth pastor about the problem
- Remember that you do NOT deserve to be treated with any disrespect from others
- Pray for God's help and guidance in the situation.

Be of Good Courage!

Whatever you do, you need courage. Whatever course you decide upon, there is always someone to tell you that you are wrong. There are always difficulties arising that tempt you to believe your critics are right. To map out a course of action and follow it to an end requires some of the same courage that a soldier needs.

> Peace has its victories, but it takes brave men and women to win them.
>
> Ralph Waldo Emerson

"Don't be afraid, for I am with you. Do not be dismayed, for I am your God. I will strengthen you. I will help you. I will uphold you with My victorious right hand." *Isaiah 41:10 NLT*

GET A GRIP ... GOD IS WITH YOU!

Cool Thought:
Faith is taking the first step even when you don't see the staircase.

Martin Luther King, Jr.

Tips/Advice:

Always be careful when you deal with someone who may try to harm you in any way. Never attempt to take care of those matters alone. Even David had the backing of thousands of warriors as he went out to face the giant, Goliath. Your Goliath may be more than you can handle and that's okay. You are surrounded by those who care about you and are ready to help you. Just let them know what you need and keep your faith, your family, and your friends close by your side.

DEAR GOD, I simply don't understand why someone who barely knows me wants to make my life miserable. Please help me to trust those who can help me get past people who are mean spirited. Please strengthen me to deal with the things I don't understand. Thank You for being there for me. AMEN.

One's philosophy is not best expressed in words; it is expressed in the choices one makes. In the long run, we shape our lives and we shape ourselves. The process never ends until we die. And the choices we make are ultimately our responsibility.

Eleanor Roosevelt

BLESSINGS FROM GOD AT SCHOOL

Now that we've gotten through the squabbles with our siblings at home and with some bullies out there in the world, let's look at some of the great blessings that God has for you at school. Maybe you haven't stopped to think about your school experience as having anything to do with the way your life may shape in the future, but it's worth a thought. What you do now, today, can make all the difference in the direction of your life down the road. Consider the kinds of choices you have to make.

The Game Is On! Be Choosey!

I have set before you life and death, blessing and cursing; therefore choose life, that both you and your descendants may live.

Deuteronomy 30:19 NKJV

Be part of the team. Go it alone. Everything you do is about making a choice and that will never change. Your choices will always be up to you. You will always have to own them.

Cool Thought:
Every moment you have a choice,
regardless of what has happened before.
Choose right now to move forward, positively
and confidently into your incredible future.

No matter where you go to school, you're surrounded by experiences that influence the way you think, the way you dress, and the way you perceive the world and relationships. You learn to embrace or reject being part of the team, or part of the leadership of your school, or part of its social life. You have the opportunity to make a difference, and your beliefs about yourself and your faith in God can strengthen every decision you make.

Let's see what God's blessings
are for you at school,
yes ... even at school!

Every time you make a choice you are turning the central part of you, the part that chooses, into something a little different from what it was before.

You're on a path of discovery, learning about yourself, finding what is valuable and letting go of those things that simply aren't you. You're making a lot of choices.

The gift of most schools is that you have opportunities to try a variety of things. You can discover what you're good at and what doesn't work for you. You can find out if you're meant to be on the debate team or on the soccer team or on any team at all. You can learn how it feels to cooperate with groups of people and get a sense of purpose and excitement in doing things well. You learn by doing and you learn by making an effort.

Someone close to you is watching and is counting on the very part you play. The blessing is in learning from the experience. You are the leader. You are in charge of this part of your life.

Anyone who stops learning is old, whether twenty or eighty. Anyone who keeps learning stays young. The greatest thing in life is to keep your mind young.

Henry Ford

As long as you live,
keep learning how to live.

Seneca

OPINIONS OF OTHERS MAY NOT ALWAYS SERVE YOU WELL!

Thomas Edison was sent home from school at the age of six. He bore a note to his parents explaining that he was too stupid to learn. It appears the light just didn't go on for Edison's teacher!

The ways of chemistry seemed to be overwhelming for a young man named Pasteur. His teacher was sure he'd never succeed. **Louis Pasteur** just needed more milk.

Latin seemed unbearable. In fact, he was a terrible Latin student, but that didn't stop him. He was determined to become the best student of English that he could be and **Sir Winston Churchill** began to make his mark on history with that one choice.

Think About This: You Were Designed by God

You see, it's important to know yourself, and to trust what God has designed for you. If you are still learning what your talents are, go after them, make choices that help you discover all you were meant to be. This is God's gift to you.

As you learn to become what He designed you to be, you have the chance to return His gift in full measure. That's one of the blessings of being in school.

Living and growing

offer you no guarantees ...

just choices;

no absolute certainty,

but an understanding that

there are always consequences;

no predictable outcomes ...

just the wonderful opportunity

and privilege to pursue

your dreams.

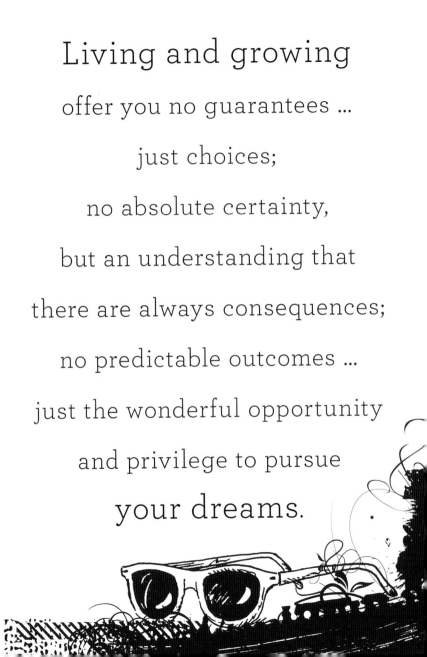

WHAT MOTIVATES YOU?

Do you love math? Can you calculate numbers in your head faster than other kids can even write down the problem? Can you solve word problems or issues in everyday situations because you have a way of looking at details and putting them together in creative and effective ways?

One of the blessings of education is just that. It helps you to define who you are and what you are good at. It helps you to focus on the things that build your character and your self-esteem. What you learn about yourself is your truth in school and it will hold true all of your life. God will continue to put you in environments where you can learn new things. Those new things will direct your paths and strengthen your heart and mind.

Tips/Advice:

Make a list of things that excite you about your life right now. Maybe you'll list some interest you've discovered while taking a French class or by learning to play an instrument. Maybe you'll list how you suddenly became interested in the whole universe as you studied the solar system and realized the vastness of the stars and planets beyond our earth.

After you've made the list, find one person you trust and share your insight about yourself and what you've learned. How can you learn more? Internet searches, or online classes? Library books? Begin a project. Read, paint, study, sculpt, whatever it takes so you can learn more about the subject you're interested in. Learn so much about it that you could teach others and share your excitement with them. Always jump at the chance to learn more. It will be a blessing for a lifetime.

DEAR GOD, I thank You for my school. I thank You that You have blessed my life with so many chances to learn more about myself and to understand what You want me to be. I know I have a lot to learn, but I'm happy to discover all that You have designed for me. **Thank You. AMEN.**

BLESSINGS FROM GOD THROUGH FRIENDS

You've probably had a good friend, or perhaps a best friend since you were in grade school. A good friend understands your jokes, encourages you when you share your heart or your dreams, and stands by you when others walk away. Proverbs 18:24 says, "There is a friend who sticks closer than a brother." Yes, sometimes a good friendship is an even stronger bond than one you may have with a sibling.

Friendship is one of God's greatest blessings, whether you have a lot of friends or just one or two faithful ones. Good friends are like mirrors. They show you more about who you are. They listen to you and they hear your heart even better than they hear your words. They like you just the way you are. They reflect back to you about what they observe and what they know about you.

Cool Thought:
To have a good friend is one of the highest delights of life; to be a good friend is one of the noblest and most difficult undertakings.

Anonymous

Choosing Friends

Most of us are comfortable with people who are a lot like we are. We like to play the same games, do the same kinds of activities, and listen to the same kind of music. In fact, it's fun to hang out together for no reason at all. Good friends are a major gift to your life. Remember what Jesus called the disciples, the ones He chose to spend His three years of ministry with? He called them His friends. He chose His friends wisely and you should too.

By friendship you mean the greatest love, the greatest usefulness, the most open communication, the noblest sufferings, the severest truth, the heartiest counsel, and the greatest union of minds of which brave men and women are capable.

Jeremy Taylor

Being a Friend – It All Depends on You!

What does it take to BE a good friend? The Golden Rule applies pretty nicely here. You know, "Treat other people the way you want to be treated." Kindness, consideration, and sharing ... those are all good parts of friendship. Laughing out loud, playing sports, attending concerts, those are all good things too. But, other times you have to step back when you aren't sure you agree with what a friend is doing.

Octavia Butler said, "Sometimes being a friend means mastering the art of timing. There is a time for silence. A time to let go and allow people to hurl themselves into their own destiny. And a time to prepare to pick up the pieces when it's all over."

When you're in the midst of tough choices in a friendship, remember that you always have a chance to ask God for help. You can pray for your friend and offer comfort even when you can't offer good advice. Being a good friend doesn't mean that you always have the answers for each other. Sometimes it just means being there, being close by.

Cool Thought:
The more we love, the better we are, and the greater our friendships are, the dearer we are to God.

Jeremy Taylor

Friendship

Call, write, visit, text.

Be here now

See what's next.

Talk, listen, dance, shout,

Believe in me,

Erase my doubt.

Walk, run, stay, go,

Help me learn,

Watch me grow.

Friends like you

Are all I've got ...

How blessed I am –
I've got a lot!

True friendships
are among the
greatest
of all blessings.

The gifts of true friendships are unending. They can be unwrapped and shared, blessed, utilized and grown any time you choose. Consider the wide range of blessings you share with your friends.

Tips/Advice:

Take the opportunity to create some new friendships. Make room for someone new to come into your life and see what dimensions of learning and laughter they bring. It may take a little work to add to your friendship network, but it could be the best thing you do. Give yourself the chance to turn a stranger into a friend. It will be a blessing for you both.

DEAR GOD, I'm happy that I have been blessed with good friends. I know that there are others in my school or church that might also be good friends if I just let them in. Help me to be open to new possibilities even in my friendships. Thank You, Lord, for being an everlasting friend to me. **AMEN.**

Sticking with it:
The Blessings of God When We Persevere

Do you ever think to yourself that it might just be easier to quit? To give up? Have you tried out for the team three times and failed, or applied for the year book staff and have still not been selected? Have you run for Student Council or class secretary, but never won? Whatever you try in life, only one thing can get you to the goal and that's perseverance. There's just no short cut that will work.

We are hard pressed on every side, but not crushed; perplexed, but not in despair; persecuted, but not abandoned; struck down, but not destroyed.

2 Corinthians 4:8-9

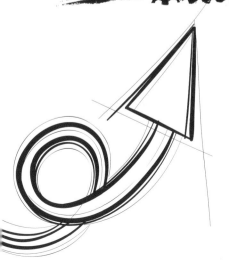

What a Winner Does

How many times does a winner go back to try again? That's easy. Until he wins! You're a winner too. You've been blessed by God to do wonderful stuff and you've got the talent to do it. If the door keeps closing on something you've set your heart toward, then you have a choice.

You can keep refining and honing your skills, get better at it and try again, or you can look at the effort as one that directs you to try something else. Maybe you're not going to be the captain of the basketball team, but you might be the best volleyball player the school has ever seen. You might have to take your skills to another level or in a new direction.

What's the Difference?

The difference between a successful person and others is not a lack of strength, nor a lack of knowledge, but rather a lack of will.

Vince Lombardi

God loves it when you make an effort. He applauds you by giving you the desire to keep trying. He motivates others to help you achieve your goals. He sees you at your worst and brings you back to a stronger sense of optimism. You are not alone in your efforts.

Perseverance isn't a matter of preparing for a long race. You don't have to get into the marathon to win. You just have to be ready to run, to sprint, to keep going when the odds seem to be against you. You have to try to win the small races, one right after another.

We know that with God all things are possible. Brother Lawrence said, "All things are possible to him who believes, yet more to him who hopes, more still to him who loves, and most of all to him who practices and perseveres in these three virtues."

SO WHERE IS YOUR FOCUS?

Here's a personal story. Once in my prayer time, I was quietly walking behind Jesus, going up the path leading to a mountain. He got ahead of me and I soon noticed this giant boulder in the road. It was taller than I was and blocked my view of Jesus. Jesus was already way up ahead. I started to worry that I wouldn't be able to get past the boulder. It was all that I could see. I called out to Jesus to stop and help me. It took a little time, but He finally realized I was not right behind Him so He turned around. He could just barely see me jumping up and down behind the big rock.

He smiled and started walking back in my direction. As He got closer to me, I noticed one incredible thing. He kept getting bigger as I focused on Him. By the time He got to me, all I could see was Him! The boulder was now the size of a pebble. Jesus picked it up and showed it to me. Then He threw it over His shoulder.

The lesson to me was this. Keep my focus on Jesus and not on the obstacles and everything will be okay. The lesson is the same for you. Keep your eyes on Him!

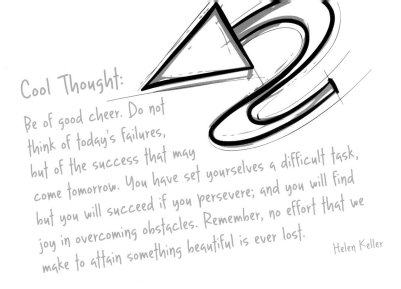

Cool Thought:

Be of good cheer. Do not think of today's failures, but of the success that may come tomorrow. You have set yourselves a difficult task, but you will succeed if you persevere; and you will find joy in overcoming obstacles. Remember, no effort that we make to attain something beautiful is ever lost.

Helen Keller

Tips/Advice

When you're feeling discouraged, go online and look at stories of people who have overcome incredible odds to succeed. Read about them, imagine yourself in their shoes, and give yourself credit for all the efforts you've made. Make a list of all the successes you've already had so you can remind yourself of what it feels like to win. You're already a success. You already have many reasons to be proud. Reward yourself when you accomplish a goal no matter what the outcome may be.

DEAR GOD, I'm tired. I feel like I've been trying and trying to make the most of the talents You gave me. So far, I can't really see where it's getting me. Please help me not to quit. Help me to know that You are right beside me and that You already see that there's an open door up ahead.

Thank You, Lord. **AMEN.**

Look at this:

By perseverance
the snail reached the ark!

Charles H. Spurgeon

BECOMING THE MOST EXCELLENT YOU!

You're the star of your own reality show. That's right. You and a cast of characters you call friends are creating a buzz, calling attention to yourself in ways that will serve you well or will leave you wondering just what happened. When you stay tuned in to the Creator of your soul, you have the most excellent possibility of becoming all He meant you to become. You're not in a dress rehearsal for your life, you're already in prime time and how you play your part, create your role, and connect to your audience is going to make all the difference.

Being a Teenager Doesn't Mean God Can't Use You Right Now!

How do you want others to see you? What do you want to give and what do you hope to gain from where you stand right now? If you think that being a teenager dismisses you from needing to care about these things, take another look and go to the One who made you for some extra insight. It's always your time to shine!

Excellence is an art won by training and habituation. We do not act rightly because we have virtue or excellence, but we rather have those because we have acted rightly.

We are what we repeatedly do. Excellence, then, is not an act but a habit.

Aristotle

In everything, set them an example by doing what is good.

Titus 2:7

Tips/Advice:

Take some time to create a self-portrait. Look in the mirror and make a note of what you see. Be truthful. Be yourself and see if you discover anything that you might not have realized. Do you believe that you see yourself the way others see you? Are you showing the world the most excellent person you can be? Go ahead, make a drawing or a painting of the person you see now. Six months from now, try it again and see if you notice how you've grown and changed.

Cool Thought:
The quality of a person's life is in direct proportion to their commitment to excellence, regardless of their chosen field of endeavor.

Vince Lombardi

DEAR GOD, Thank You for making me, me. I am learning more all the time about what that means and I'm growing every day. Help me to be honest about who I am today and who I want to be. Help me to be a person of excellence. Help me to be someone of whom You can be proud even though I'm still a teenager. **AMEN.**

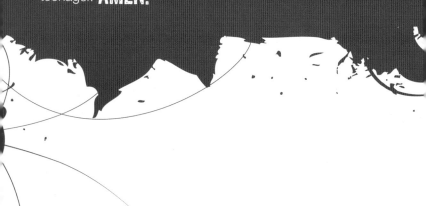

BLESSINGS FROM GOD IN RELATIONSHIPS

You're always in a relationship. You may like a certain person at school and hope that you can develop a social relationship, even go on a date or become best friends. You may have a job after school and so you have a relationship with your boss. You have a relationship at home with your father, your mother, and each sibling and all of those relationships are different. You have a relationship with God. The fact is that you have a slightly different way of behaving with nearly every person you meet. So what does God want from you in terms of a relationship? What does He expect from you?

"Those whom I love I rebuke and discipline. So be earnest, and repent. Here I am! I stand at the door and knock. If anyone hears My voice and opens the door, I will come in and eat with him, and he with Me."

Revelation 3:19-20

Do you know that you can actually spend time "hanging out" with God? Yes, you can! You can take your lunch and go sit quietly and talk to Him about everything that's important to you. You can tell Him about your grades or your disappointment over something you've done. You can tell Him about the person you're attracted to or why you're not too fond of your English teacher. You can do that because you actually have a living relationship with the King of the Universe. He sees you. He knows you. He loves you. You're His kid!

When you "hang out" with God, He gets a chance to share some of His best stuff with you! He gets a chance to share more about His hopes for you too.

Every personal relationship you have requires one thing from you. You have to be willing to risk your heart and even to be vulnerable. When you do, you begin to grow, to develop a sense of what it means to be connected to others in positive ways. You can let go of that uneasy sense that you're somehow here all on your own.

The fact is that you were made for relationships.

A Prodigal Story

If you're not sure how all this works, go back and read the story of the prodigal son (Luke 15). Remember how things worked out for him? In this amended version from the text, the son had chosen to take his inheritance and leave his father's house.

He squandered all the money playing video games and creating meaningless relationships with loose friends. He ended up with nothing and had to rummage through garbage cans to find food. Then one day, he started thinking about home again. He thought he might be able to eat better if he could convince his father to just let him back in the door. He'd even get a job at Burger King and pay his father back some of the money he had wasted. So he headed home.

But here's the good news! Just as the son was coming around the bend on a borrowed motorcycle from a friend, his father saw him coming. He dropped everything and started running. He ran to his son. They collapsed in each other's arms and the son begged for forgiveness. You see, the father didn't care as much about what the son had done wrong, as he cared about the son. He loved his son. In the same way, God loves you.

So, you see, the father had already forgiven him. After the hugs, the father called the whole family together and they had a big feast to celebrate. After all, his son had come home again. It's a tear-jerker, a moment to be savored.

Looking for God?

Whoever walks toward God even a foot or two, will instantly discover that God runs toward him as fast as He can. This is one of God's greatest blessings. He is running toward you right now.

Tips/Advice

Think about the people you choose to hang out with. What are the benefits of your friendship with them? What are the drawbacks? Which of your current relationships gives you the greatest chance to simply be yourself? Create a list of all your relationships and then take a pen and assign each one a number of 1, 2, or 3. Give them a **1** if the relationship benefits both of you in nearly every way. Give them a **2** if it's a newer relationship, or one that is more outside your usual circle. Give them a **3** if you aren't sure why you're even friends with this person or if you can see that they actually have a negative impact on you. If you've assigned a **3** to anyone on your list, it may be time to change things or move on. What number did you assign to God?

DEAR GOD, I know that I don't talk to You nearly as much as I should. I know You are always there for me, but sometimes I try too hard to take everything on by myself. It makes me feel more in charge when I do that. Help me remember that You are right here and that it's a whole lot better if I just let You be in control. Thanks for listening to me. **AMEN.**

God's Blessings on Your Creativity

You may not always see this, but you rock! You've got talent! You've got the music in you and God loves to see you dance. There's nothing He likes better than watching you get in touch with all that makes you unique. You are a one-of-a-kind design and God has His fingerprint on you. You are His workmanship. Now what will you do with all that talent?

> **O, Lord, You are our Father. We are the clay, You are the potter; we are all the work of Your hand.**
>
> Isaiah 64:8 NLT

In God, You Get to Be a Free Spirit!

When someone plays by their own rules or takes life on in a unique way, we sometimes call that person a "free spirit." We think of them as having a different set of rules to go by than other people have. Creative people are often in that mix. The child prodigy who plays like Mozart at age 3 or the young actor who wins an Oscar before the age of 12 makes us think that these people are more special than we are. The truth is you have been blessed to be a free spirit too. Your spirit is entwined with the living Source of all good, the one real Spirit in this universe.

You are free to be all you can be because of Him. Now, that's really being a free spirit.

When God created you, He had a plan in mind. He knew exactly what you would become and what your purpose would be. He took the clay that is you and molded and shaped it and designed it to be perfect. The fact is He is still willing to shape and mold you as you stay in relationship with Him so that you become a person of both purpose and excellence. You couldn't have a better mentor.

You are poised for an Oscar-winning performance.

The Truth Will Set You Free

Jesus told His followers in John 8 that the truth would set them free and He meant it. You are free! You are free to think bigger, to create more, to forgive, to laugh, to love and to embrace all you are meant to be. You may be a teenager today, but you are forming the basis of the kind of person you will be the rest of your life. These are some of the most blessed years you'll ever experience. Hold them close. They will disappear soon enough.

Cool Thought:
If you don't learn and know your truths, you cannot speak them. If you don't speak them, you will know a prison within. Tell your truths to yourself, and then to others. The truth really will set you free!

Truth is the greatest gift of life and love is the exercise of that truth.

Tips/Advice:

Pick three friends and sit down together. Take turns giving three examples of what you believe makes that other person unique. Talk about each other's talents, ways of handling life, ways of being a friend that you find especially helpful. Build each other up and help strengthen each other to keep trying to be all you were meant to be. When each person has had a turn, take one of the special things mentioned about you and see what you can do to make a good thing even better. How can you grow from what you know now to be the talents and gifts that God has given you?

DEAR GOD, I thank You for giving me the gifts I have. I don't always see them, but I thank You that others can see them and that I can learn from their views of me. Help me to make the most of the cool ways You have worked in my life. AMEN.

GOD'S BLESSINGS FOR YOU WHEREVER YOU ARE!

There are changes ahead. Some things will happen to you that you never would have dreamed of. Some dreams will happen that you didn't make big enough. Some things will feel like answers to prayer and you may not even remember whether you prayed about them or not. God knows what you need. He runs to meet you. He answers even before you call Him.

God set you in a family, in a home, in an environment where you could learn and grow and become the uniquely wonderful person He meant you to become. He is proud of you and believes in you.

God Knows You're a Star!

God watches over you when others try to tempt you in the wrong direction or bully you into an unfair advantage. He wants you to be cool, to persist, to try over and over again because He already knows what a star you are. He wants you to remember Him in everything you do and give yourself another chance when you fail.

God wants a daily relationship with you. The more time you spend with Him, the more He knows you, understands your heart, and the more He can do for you. You're His, inside and out.

Francis de Sales said this,

"Do not look forward to the changes and chances of this life in fear; rather look to them with full hope that, as they arise, God, whose you are, will deliver you out of them. He is your keeper. He has kept you up till now. Hold fast to His dear hand, and He will lead you safely through all things; and, when you cannot stand, He will bear you in His arms. Do not look forward to what may happen tomorrow. Our Father will either shield you from suffering, or He will give you strength to bear it."

He guides me

The Lord is my shepherd, I shall not be in want. He makes me lie down in green pastures, He leads me beside quiet waters, He restores my soul. He guides me in paths of righteousness for His name's sake. Even though I walk through the valley of the shadow of death, I will fear no evil, for You are with me; Your rod and Your staff, they comfort me.

You prepare a table before me in the presence of my enemies. You anoint my head with oil; my cup overflows. Surely goodness and love will follow me all the days of my life, and I will dwell in the house of the Lord forever.

Psalm 23, NKJV

God's blessings are all based on one important thing. It's all about love. You're blessed because you're loved. You're God's child, His workmanship, His creation and He adores you. If you were the only being on this planet, He would have sent Jesus to walk with you and to save you. He would have done all of this out of love.

As you go forward, let all you do be out of love. Love yourself, love your family, and love others who come into your life and walk away again. They are all meant to be there for a time.

They are all part of God's plan to help you learn and grow. **GOD HAS UNCONDITIONAL LOVE FOR YOU.** He wants to teach you to love in the same way.

Cool Thought:
You will find, as you look back upon your life, that the moments when you really lived are the moments when you have done things in the spirit of love.

Henry Drummond

Tips/Advice:

Write down the top ten things that you would say you love. Assign a number to each one according to its importance. Make number one the most important, and number ten the least important. What can you do to love what you listed as number one even more? What can you do to move number ten up on the chart? What isn't there that you could add now? This list will help you identify the things that mean the most to you. These are your passions in life. They may change or become more defined as you grow older. They may not. They are still important to you now.

DEAR GOD, thank You for walking with me each day. Thank You for talking with me and guiding me through school and work and with my friends. I know that You are watching over me all the time. Help me to be the best me possible. I want to make You proud. **AMEN.**

Jesus Loves Me for Teens
(You can even sing it if you'd like.)

Jesus loves me
this I know
'Cause He's cool
and tells me so,
Even when I do things wrong,
He forgives
and makes me strong.
Yes, Jesus loves me.
Yes, Jesus loves me.
Yes, Jesus loves me.
He always will, I know.

Love
is all we have,
the only way that
each can help the other.

Euripides